T0365900

# FUSION SAFARI

## BY MEAGHAN HILL

All photographs and images produced in this
book created and/or processed by Richard White
of Sundance Photography (https://sundance.
photography/)

Print information available on the last page

Rev. date: 12/15/2017

To order additional copies of this book, contact:
Xlibris
1-800-455-039
www.xlibris.com.au
Orders@Xlibris.com.au

# This book is dedicated to

## Prosper Taruvinga

## From Livelong Digital

(www.livelongdigital.com.au)

Thanks for everything mate

# INTRODUCTION

The reason I've chosen to do this cookbook, is to try and bring people from different backgrounds together. The world we currently live in is not a happy one, there's too much hate. What we need to do is start again with the basics, and food is a basic. Food also brings people together, and that's the aim of this book.

The brain knows that spices from different countries can come together and create awesome dishes. I believe that the heart needs a reminder that people can also come together to achieve greatness.

For years I've been fascinated with everything African. Her people, her languages, her cultures, her colours and her food. I've found that African's cook with a wide range of spices, most of which are found in our own kitchen cupboards.

I've taken some dishes that I enjoy and added my version of an African twist to each. I thought what better way to honour such remarkable people and breath-taking flavours, then to redesign some of my favourite dishes.

So; let me take you on a journey around the world, where you will discover new tastes and mind-blowing flavours. I want to take you to a place where the aromas of different flavours will fill your kitchen and your soul with love.

# CONTENTS

# CHUTNEYS

## Paw Pawlicious

## Ingredients

200g diced Pawpaw
200g brown sugar
150ml Apple cider vinegar
1 teaspoon crushed ginger
1 tablespoon West African pepper soup mix (see West African Pepper Soup Mix)
100g tomato paste
20mls olive oil

## Method

Heat oil in a large saucepan over a low-medium heat. Add diced pawpaw and ginger. Cook for 5 minutes, stirring occasionally.

Add remaining ingredients and stir. Cook without letting it boil until sugar dissolves.

Turn heat down to low and simmer uncovered for approximately 20 minutes, stirring occasionally.

Pour into sterilised jars, or in containers in the fridge. (Will keep in fridge for a couple weeks)

Makes approximately 500g

# Mango Bomb

## Ingredients

800g tin mangoes, drained
1 small brown onion, finely diced
1 teaspoon crushed garlic and ginger
500mls white wine vinegar
220g white sugar
½ teaspoon mixed spice, ground allspice, ground cardamom

## Method

Bring vinegar, sugar, onion, garlic, ginger and spices to the boil in a large pot. Reduce by half.

Add mango and cook for a further 10-15 minutes on low heat.

Spoon into sterilised jars, or in covered containers in the fridge. Will keep in fridge for a few weeks.

Makes approximately 600g

# Feisty Date

## Ingredients

500g pitted dates, roughly chopped
1 teaspoon Chinese 5 spice, Moroccan spice
1 tablespoon dried chilli flakes
20mls olive oil
1 tablespoon crushed garlic
180g firmly packed brown sugar
750mls brown vinegar
500mls water

## Method

Heat oil in a large pot over a medium heat.

Add Moroccan spice, Chinese 5 spice and garlic.

Cook for 2-3 minutes, constantly stirring.

Remove from heat and add chilli flakes.

Return to heat and constantly stir for another minute, being careful not to burn the chilli.

Add dates, brown sugar, water and vinegar.

Turn heat down to low and cook until it starts to gently boil and gets sticky; stirring occasionally for 5-8 minutes.

Spoon into sterilised jars/containers in the fridge.

Makes approximately 800g.

# Flaming Tomato

## Ingredients

400g diced tomatoes
1 small brown onion, finely diced
170g firmly packed brown sugar
120mls brown vinegar
4 bay leaves, star anise
1 tablespoon Berbere mix
½ teaspoon dried chilli flakes
1 tablespoon crushed garlic
1 tablespoon olive oil

## Method

Heat oil in a medium saucepan over low heat.

Add onion and chilli flakes and cook until onion has softened, stirring occasionally for 5-7 minutes.

Add the garlic and cook for another minute.

Add diced tomatoes, brown sugar, vinegar, bay leaves, star anise and berbere mix. Stir to combine.

Increase heat to high until mixture is boiling.

Then turn heat down to low and simmer uncovered until mixture has thickened. (15-20 minutes)

Spoon into sterilised jars/containers in the fridge.

Makes approximately 450g

# SPICE BLENDS

## Berbere-Ethiopian Spice Mix

### Ingredients

1 teaspoon Turmeric
2 teaspoons ground coriander
1 teaspoon ground cumin
1 teaspoon cracked black pepper
2 teaspoons ground allspice
2 teaspoons ground cardamom
2 teaspoons ground cloves

2 teaspoons dried chilli flakes
3 teaspoons sweet paprika
1 teaspoon salt
¼ teaspoon ground nutmeg
½ teaspoon ground ginger
¼ teaspoon ground cinnamon
3 teaspoons cayenne pepper

### Method

Stir to combine

Makes approximately 84g

## Baharat-Tunisian Spice Blend

### Ingredients

Cinnamon
Dried rose petals
Cracked black pepper

### Method

I used equal amounts of all three ingredients. You can adjust to your own tastes.

# Dukkha-Egyptian Blend

## Ingredients

110g ground hazelnuts
80g ground sesame seeds
2 tablespoons ground mint
2 tablespoons ground coriander

2 tablespoons ground cumin
2 tablespoons cracked black pepper
1 tablespoon salt

## Method

Mix to combine

Makes approximately 220g

# Ras El Hanout

## Ingredients

1 teaspoon ground ginger
1 teaspoon ground cumin
1 teaspoon salt
¾ teaspoon cracked black pepper

½ teaspoon ground allspice
¼ teaspoon ground cloves
½ teaspoon ground cinnamon
½ teaspoon cayenne pepper

## Method

Mix together all the ingredients in a small bowl until well combined.

Makes approximately 16g

# West African Pepper Soup Mix

## Ingredients

20g - ground black pepper
20g - ground cloves
20g - ground cinnamon
20g - ground nutmeg
10g - ground coriander

10g - ground cumin
10g - ground ginger
10g - ground fennel seeds
10g – tamarind powder

## Method

Mix all together well.

Makes 130g

# Ayib-Ethiopian Cheese

## Ingredients

600mls buttermilk
1 litre full cream milk
2 teaspoons salt
Cheesecloth / really thick paper towel

## Method

Combine milk, buttermilk and salt in a large heavy bottomed pot over high heat; until mixture has separated into white curds and translucent whey. This will take 8-10 minutes, don't stir.

Take pot off the heat and let it stand for 3 minutes after separation. This is so the curds cling together and facilitate the straining step.

Line a colander with cheesecloth/paper towel. Make sure the paper towel is of good quality so it doesn't tear easily.

Ladle contents into prepared colander and let the whey drain. 1-2 minutes.

Lift the four corners of cheesecloth/paper towel and gather together. Gently twist and press out excess whey, being very careful because it will be very hot. Unwrap.

Can be served immediately or cooled to room temperature.

If refrigerating, wrap in cling wrap and it will keep up to two days. Stand for ten minutes at room temperature before serving.

# Pumpkin And Yam Puree

## Ingredients

300g pumpkin, cut into small pieces
300g yam, cut into small pieces
Water to cover pumpkin and yam.

## Method

Put pumpkin, yam and water into a medium sized pot. Cook on a high heat until water starts to boil.

Turn heat down to low and simmer until mixture is cooked.

Spoon mixture into a blender and blend until mixture is puréed.

# Béchamel

## Ingredients

100g butter
½ cup plain flour
5 cups milk

## Method

Melt butter in a small pot over a medium heat.

Remove from heat and add flour. Whisk together to make a roux.

Add ⅕ of the milk and stir constantly until mixture starts to thicken.

Turn heat down to low and add another ⅕ of milk. Stir occasionally until it starts to thicken again.

Repeat this process until all the milk has been used and mixture is thick and glossy.

# BREAKFASTS

## Tunisian-Style French Toast with Almond Ice Cream

### Ingredients-serves 2

2 eggs
40mls cream
1 tsp Baharat spice blend
Almond ice cream
2 pieces of 1-inch bread
Icing sugar

## Method

Whisk egg and cream together. Add Baharat spice mix.

Dip each slice of bread into egg mixture. Cook on a hot grill/frypan. Cook for 2-3 minutes until golden brown. Flip with a spatula and cook until other side is also golden brown.

Cut each slice diagonally and place two slices on each plate.

Dust with icing sugar. Serve with almond ice cream.

# Meaghan's Stack

## Ingredients- serves 4

1 lemon cut into wedges
4 eggs
400g haloumi, sliced
1 roasted capsicum, sliced
Water
¼ cup white vinegar
300g sliced mushrooms

Dukkah
80-100g rocket/spinach
Mint paste
1 tsp harissa spice mix
Oil
1 tablespoon butter

## Method

Fry slices haloumi on each side until golden brown. Meanwhile, bring a pot of water and vinegar to the boil.

Melt butter in a frypan and cook mushrooms for 2-3mins. Add harissa and cook for another 3-5mins until mushrooms are cooked.

Using a large spoon, stir the boiling water anti-clockwise. Break eggs and cook to your liking.

Place ½ tsp of mint paste into each 'corner' of each plate.

Roll rocket/spinach into balls and place in the middle of each plate. Layer each plate with capsicum, haloumi and mushrooms.

Place a poached egg on each plate. Place a lemon wedge on each plate and serve.

# Meaghan's Smoked Salmon and Avocado Smash with Lemon and Dill Dressing

## Ingredients- serves 2

Smoked salmon slices
2 avocados
⅓ cup ayib cheese
½ tsp dill

¼ cup lemon juice
2 mini ciabatta/Turkish breads
¼ cup olive oil
Salt and pepper to taste

For the Dressing: Whisk ¾ of the lemon juice, oil and dill until combined

## Method

Mix avocado and ayib together until it resembles 'avo smash.' Add rest of lemon juice, then salt and pepper to taste.

Toast the bread. Spread the smashed avocado onto each part of the toast. Roll up salmon pieces and place on top.

Drizzle the dressing on top and serve.

# Moroccan Extravaganza

## Ingredients- serves 2

¼ tsp dukkah
2 Turkish bread portions
4 eggs
60mls cream
300g sliced mushrooms

Handful of spinach
1 Tablespoon butter
Olive oil
1 tablespoons Moroccan spice
1 tomato, diced

## Method

Melt butter in a hot pan. Add mushrooms and tomato and cook for 2-3mins.

Add Moroccan spice and cook for a further 2mins. Once cooked, toss through spinach- being careful not to overcook spinach.

Meanwhile, whisk egg and cream together. Melt butter in another pan and add the egg mix, whisking until eggs are cooked.

Toast the Turkish bread and place in the middle of each plate. Add the mushroom mix on top, followed by the egg.

Sprinkle dukkah on top and serve.

# North African Inspired Lamb Eggs Benedict

## Ingredients- serves 2

4 eggs
Fresh rocket
½ purple onion, sliced
½ capsicum, sliced
200g Lamb, cut into strips
2 tablespoons Harissa

1 Turkish bread, cut in half
Olive oil
¼ cup vinegar
Water
½ cup Paw Pawlicious chutney

## Method

Heat oil in a pan and cook onion and capsicum. Add harissa and cook until onion is soft.
Add lamb and cook to your liking.

In a small pot, boil water and vinegar. With a perforated spoon, stir water in a clockwise motion. Break the eggs into the water and cook for 2-3 minutes. Using the perforated spoon, spoon eggs out and drain on paper towel.

Toast the Turkish bread and place half on each plate. Place the rocket on each bread. Add the lamb mixture, then the poached eggs. Pipe the Paw Pawlicious chutney on top and serve.

# VEGETARIAN

## Vegetarian Pasta

### Ingredients- serves 6

500g cooked fettuccine
250g sliced mushrooms
1 large purple onion, roughly chopped
1 zucchini, cut into batons
1 eggplant, cut into batons
1 capsicum, cut into batons
300g Flaming Tomato Chutney

Olive oil

## Method

Heat oil in a large wok and sauté onions for 3-4 minutes. Turn heat down to low. Add vegetables and cook for approximately 5 minutes.

Add jar of Flaming Tomato Chutney and simmer for a couple more minutes.

Add pasta and toss through.

Serve

# Spicy Bean Chilli

## Ingredients- serves 6

400g red kidney beans
400g African black beans
400g cannelloni beans
600g diced tomatoes
350g tomato paste
50mls water
1 tablespoon dried chilli flakes
1 tablespoon Berbere mix

## Method

Soak beans in cold water for a minimum 6 hours. Or drain if using from a tin.

Heat oil in a large pot and cook onion on a medium heat until onion is soft. Add diced tomato, chilli flakes and Berbere mix.

Add beans, tomato paste and water. Cook on a low heat for 15-20 minutes.

Serve

# African Inspired Mushroom Risotto

## Ingredients- serves 4

600-700g sliced mushrooms
1 large brown onion, diced
170g tomato paste
4 tablespoons Ras El Hanout spice mix
1ltr vegetable stock
200g arborio rice
Olive oil

## Method

In a large pan over high heat, sauté onions for 2-3 minutes until soft.

Add mushrooms, tomato paste and Ras El Hanout spice mix and cook for 2-3 minutes.

Add rice and constantly stir so rice is well covered.

ladle of vegetable stock and stir continuously until the liquid is absorbed. Continue adding the stock at a ladleful at a time; stirring occasionally and allowing the liquid to be absorbed before adding the next ladle.

The rice should be tender, yet firm to the bite.

Spoon into bowls and serve.

# East African Inspired Lentils with Damper

## Ingredients – serves 4

2 medium brown onions, diced
2 teaspoons crushed garlic
1 teaspoon crushed ginger
 370g red lentils
½ teaspoon ground cloves
½ teaspoon ground cardamom
Dried chilli flakes (optional)
Olive oil

## Method

Heat oil in a large pot over medium-high heat. Sauté onion, garlic and ginger for 3-5 minutes, stirring occasionally.

Add lentils, cloves and cardamom. Fill pot with water-6cm above level of lentils. Bring to a boil, then turn down to a simmer to finish cooking. (The longer the lentils cook, the mushier it gets)

Serve on its own, or with toast

# East Meets West Vegetarian Lasagne

## Ingredients- serves 8

500g eggplant, sliced
1 zucchini, sliced
1/8 pumpkin, sliced
500g sweet potato, peeled and sliced
500g sliced mushrooms
250g spinach
Lasagne sheets
¼ cup balsamic vinegar

Bechamel sauce-see page 17
400g diced tomato
200g tomato paste
40g mixed herbs
Grated cheese
1 purple onion, thinly sliced
1 large brown onion, finely diced
1 tablespoon crushed garlic

Ground coriander, Chinese 5 spice, Cumin, Moroccan and Harissa. (Enough to coat the vegetables)

Olive oil
Coat the vegetables with the following spices-

| | |
|---|---|
| Eggplant - Harissa | Pumpkin - cumin |
| Zucchini - coriander | Sweet potato - Chinese 5 spice |

## Method

Pre-heat oven to 180c

Cook each vegetable on a medium/high grill or frypan for a few minutes each side until tender, not mushy.

Meanwhile, heat oil in a large pot over high heat. Sauté onion and garlic for 3-5 minutes, stirring occasionally.

Add tomato paste, diced tomatoes and mixed herbs. Cook for 5-7 minutes.

Cook mushrooms with a little oil and Moroccan seasoning.

Cook purple onion with balsamic vinegar until onion is soft.

Grease a tray with cooking spray.

Lay the eggplant as the base, spoon some Napoli on top.

Add a layer of lasagne sheets.

Lay down zucchini, followed by Napoli and béchamel and another layer of lasagne sheets.

Lay down spinach, then pumpkin and sweet potato on top, followed by more Napoli, béchamel and lasagne sheets.

Last layers are mushrooms, caramelised onions, Napoli, béchamel and grated cheese.

Cook in oven for approximately 40-45 minutes.

Serve with salad/chips

# POULTRY

## African Inspired Satay Chicken

### Ingredients- serves 4

600g diced chicken
¼ cup firmly packed brown sugar
2 tablespoons chilli flakes
500g Crunchy peanut butter
2 tablespoons crushed garlic
300mls coconut cream

½ teaspoon oyster sauce
100g yam diced
1 bunch bok choy
20mls olive oil
400g basmati rice, cooked
170g tomato paste

½ teaspoon curry powder

1 tablespoons crushed ginger

¼ teaspoon ground cloves

100mls water

1 teaspoon ground cumin

## Method

Heat oil and cook garlic and ginger for a few minutes.

Add yam and water and cook for a further five minutes. Add chicken, tomato paste, cumin, chilli and cloves. Stir until combined.

Meanwhile, whisk peanut butter, coconut cream, oyster sauce, curry powder and brown sugar. Mix well and add to chicken.

Cook for a further 10-15 minutes until chicken is cooked.

Serve with rice

# Crispy Style Peri-Peri Duck

## Ingredients- serves 2

1 duck cut in half, butterflied
¼ cup olive oil
2 limes, zested and juiced
1 lemon, zested and juiced
2 tablespoons firmly packed brown sugar
3 tablespoons ras el hanout spice
Salad/vegetables

## Method

Combine oil, lemon, lime, brown sugar and ras el hanout. Mix well.

Place the duck skin side down in a large bowl and rub the marinade over the duck. Turn duck over and rub with marinade. Allow the duck to marinate for up to 24hrs.

Pre-heat oven to 190°C. Place the duck into a baking dish and cook for approx. 1 hour. Baste frequently with marinade.

Allow duck to cook 10-15mins before serving with salad or vegetables.

# German and South African Inspired Duck Stew

## Ingredients – serves 4

2 ducks, cut into quarters
1 small onion, sliced
100g Sauerkraut
2 tablespoons duck fat
2 cups of dried apricots, roughly chopped
4 tablespoons Ras El Hanout spice blend
4 cups shredded cabbage
4 cups cooked rice
1 litre vegetable stock

## Method

Heat duck fat in a large pot over medium high heat. Brown the duck the duck well especially on skin side. Transfer to a plate

Once done, add onion and cabbage to pot and sauté for 3-5mins.

Turn heat to low.

Add sauerkraut, stock and spices. Nestle the duck in the middle and baste with a little of the liquid. Cover and simmer over low heat for approx. 1hr, adding the apricots after 40mins.

Place rice in the centre of each plate. Divide the duck onto each plate and serve.

# North African Inspired Chicken Pilaf Surprise with Orange Juice

## Ingredients-serves 4

1 large brown onion
1 tablespoon crushed garlic
2 tablespoons olive oil
200g slivered almonds
150g sultanas

3 tablespoons Moroccan spice
600g diced chicken breast
4 cups of cooked basmati rice
¾ cup orange juice

## Method

In a large pan, heat oil and cook onion and garlic until onion is soft.

Add Moroccan spice and chicken. Cook until chicken is browned.

Turn heat down to low.

Add almonds and sultanas and cook for approximately 10-15 minutes until chicken is cooked.

Add cooked basmati rice and mix well.

Ladle into bowls and drizzle orange juice over the top.

Serve.

# RED MEAT

## Ethiopian Inspired Beef Lasagne

## Ingredients- serves 8

1 onion
2 tablespoons crushed garlic
500g beef mince
250g Lasagne sheets
170g tomato paste
1 tablespoon Berbere mix
30g mixed herbs
400g diced tomatoes
500g grated cheese
Olive oil
Bechamel sauce-see page 17.

## Method

Pre-heat oven to 180°C.

Heat oil in a large pot over medium heat. Cook onion and garlic for 2-3 minutes. Add mince and cook until mince is browned.

Add diced tomatoes, tomato paste, mixed herbs and Berbere mix. Cook for 10-15 minutes.

Grease a baking dish and put down a layer of red mince, enough to cover the base.

Ladle a cup of béchamel on top and spread it over the mince.

Put down a layer of lasagne sheets.

Repeat process until all the mince, béchamel and lasagne sheets are finished.

Cook in pre-heated oven for 40-45 minutes.

Serve with salad.

# Thai Beef Salad with Spicy Date Chutney

## Ingredients – serves 4

100-150g Feisty Date Chutney
Mixed lettuce
1 Cucumber, deseeded
10 Mint leaves, thinly sliced
1 medium Purple onion, thinly sliced
100g Cherry tomatoes, halved
400-450g beef, thinly sliced
Water

## Method

Divide chutney into two bowls. Mix water with both. (Add water slowly until you get consistency you desire)

Marinate beef with half of the chutney and cook to your liking.

Toss the rest of ingredients together to make a salad. Divide onto plates.

Place beef on top then drizzle rest of chutney

# Beef Burger

## Ingredients- serves 2

150g Beef Mince
1 egg
¼ cup breadcrumbs
1 tablespoon Moroccan seasoning
¼ cup Dry slaw
2 tablespoons Japanese mayo
2 Serves Turkish bread
2 slices cheese
1 tablespoon olive oil

2 tablespoons Flaming Tomato chutney

## Method

Mix mince, egg, Moroccan seasoning and breadcrumbs. Roll into two patties.

Heat oil and cook patties for a few min each side.

Meanwhile, mix the dry slaw and Japanese mayo.

Toast the Turkish bread and put on a board.

Put the dry slaw mix on the bottom part of

The bread. Spread the Flaming Tomato on

The top half of the bread.

Place the beef patty on top of the dry slaw and add a slice of cheese on top. Place the top half the bread and serve.

# East African Inspired Succulent Lamb Cutlets

## Ingredients- serves 4

16 lamb cutlets
200g cooked rice
400g garden salad
6-8 tablespoons breadcrumbs
6-8 tablespoons mint paste
6-8 tablespoons Berbere mix
Olive oil

## Method

Preheat oven to 170°C.

Rub each cutlet with Berbere mix, then mint paste, then breadcrumbs.

In a large frypan, heat oil over a low heat. Seal each side of the lamb. (1-2 minutes)

Wrap foil around each bone before putting in the oven to finish cooking (5-7 minutes)

Divide salad and rice into each plate. Arrange lamb over the rice and serve.

# Goat Stew

## Ingredients- serves 4

650-700g goat meat, cut into bite sized pieces
1 jar Flaming Tomato Chutney
4 cups cooked long grain rice
Water
½ cup vinegar
Olive oil

## Method

Boil water and vinegar. Add goat meat and half cook (vinegar tenderises the goat)

Drain goat. Heat some oil in a pot and add goat and Flaming Tomato Chutney. Finish cooking goat on a low heat.

Spoon rice into bowls and ladle stew on top.

Serve.

# SEAFOOD

## North African Style Baby Octopus

### Ingredients- serves 4

2 litres olive oil
800g frozen octopus
100g Harissa
85g mixed herbs
100mls white vinegar
Lemons
Water

## Method – Baby Octopus

Place frozen octopus in a large heavy bottomed pot. Fill with water, vinegar and half the Harissa. Add lemons and cook on a medium heat until tender. Drain.

Mix oil, rest of Harissa and mixed herbs together. Add octopus and more lemons. Cover and refrigerate overnight or minimum 4 hours.

Heat up a large frypan/grill. Strain octopus and cook on a high heat for approximately 8-10 minutes until crispy; tossing occasionally.

Place on plate with Meaghan's Special Salad.

Serve.

# Meaghan's Special Salad

## Ingredients – serves 4

300g mixed rocket and spinach
250g Roma tomatoes, halved
2 avocados, cut into mini cubes
1 continental cucumber, de-seeded and sliced on an angle
½ red onion, thinly sliced
2 tablespoons chopped mint
100g marinated peppers

## Method – Meaghan's Special Salad

Toss all ingredients in a large salad bowl. Spoon onto plates.

# African Fused De-constructed Seafood Paella

## Ingredients- serves 4

1-½kg mix of calamari rings, mussels, (not in the half shell) prawns, (de-veined and
   align left and change to: headless) Barramundi, cut in bite sized pieces
1 300g jar Flaming Tomato chutney
1 tablespoon Harissa
Polenta-1 cup per person
100ml vegetable stock
1 tablespoon Tamarind paste
Olive oil
2 lemons, cut in wedges

## Method

Heat oil in a large pot on low heat. Add barramundi pieces, Tamarind paste and half of
the stock. Cook for approximately 5 minutes.

Add prawns and mussels and cook for another 2 minutes. Add Flaming Tomato Chutney and calamari rings. Cook for 3-4 minutes until all seafood is cooked (time will vary depending on how big seafood pieces are).

To cook polenta

In a deep microwave dish, add polenta and water (1 cup polenta=2 cups of water) Whisk.

Cook in microwave for 6-7 minutes. Take it out and stir. Cook for a further 3 minutes. Repeat one more time.

Whisk in Harissa and cook for a further 3 minutes. The longer you cook, the firmer polenta gets.

Spoon polenta in the middle of a serving tray. Spoon seafood on/around polenta. Add lemon wedges and serve.

# Seafood Marinara with Paw Pawlicious Chutney

## Ingredients- serves 4

500g pasta
500g Marina mix
200g Paw Pawlicious Chutney
1 large brown onion
Olive oil

## Method

Bring a saucepan of water and oil to the boil. Add pasta and cook for 8 minutes. Drain.

Heat some oil in a large frypan and sauté onion for approximately 2-3 minutes.

Add Marinara mix and cook on a low-medium heat for approximately 8-10 minutes. Add Paw Pawlicious chutney and stir through. Keep cooking on a low heat until all seafood is cooked. (cooking time will vary, depending on size of seafood)

Stir through pasta and serve.

# Crispy Salmon with Burnt Butter and Tamarind Sauce

## Ingredients- serves 2

2 x 180-200g Salmon pieces, skin on
4 pieces of Broccolini
2 capsicums, de-seeded and quartered
1 tablespoon tamarind paste
50g butter
Olive oil
Salt

## Method

Score the salmon skin. Rub oil and salt into the salmon skin.

Heat some oil in a large pan over high heat. Add salmon skin side down and cook for approximately 5 minutes until skin is crispy.

Turn heat to low. Turn salmon over and finish cooking salmon to your liking.

Blanch broccolini in a small pot of water.

In a medium frying pan cook capsicum pieces over a medium heat, for a few minutes on each side.

Melt butter in a small pan until the butter is a dark brown colour, stirring once. Stir the Tamarind paste into the melted butter. Remove from heat and season with salt and pepper to taste.

Assemble all on a plate and serve.

# Chilli and Cardamom Battered Whiting with Mango Chutney

## Ingredients – serves 4

16 whiting fillets, de-boned
2 cups sifted plain flour
Soda water
1 tablespoon dried chilli flakes
1 ½ teaspoons ground cardamom
4 cups garden salad
2 capsicums, quartered and de-seeded
1 lemon, cut into wedges
Olive oil

## Method

Heat oil in a large pot over a medium heat. Time varies depending on the size of your pot and how much oil you are using.

Whisk plain flour, soda water, chilli flakes and cardamom until smooth. Dust whiting fillets in plain flour, then into the batter. Smooth one edge of each whiting on the side of the bowl and into pot of oil. Cook each fillet for 3-4 minutes. Drain on paper towel.

In a little oil in a medium frypan on low-medium heat, grill the capsicum pieces for a couple of minutes until each side is brown.

Divide garden salad and grilled capsicum over the four plates. Place 4 fillets on each plate. Serve

# DESSERTS

## Meaghan's African Style Cheese Platter

### Ingredients- serves 4

60mls olive oil
1 cup firmly packed Ayib cheese (see page AYIB-ETHIOPIAN CHEESE)
1 triangle of double Brie
100g mature cheddar
400g haloumi
100-150g crackers
70g Feisty Date Chutney

70g Flaming Tomato Chutney
500g plantain (250g fried with salt, 250g fried with cinnamon sugar)

## Method

In a large pan over high heat, heat half of the oil. Fry the haloumi for approx. 3 minutes on each side.

In another large pan over medium heat, heat the rest of the oil. Fry the plantain for 8-10 minutes on each side. Each side should be a dark brown, so don't worry you're not burning it.

Arrange cheese cuts on a cheese board / serving platter. Place the fried plantain, haloumi, crackers around the cheese. Spoon chutneys into ramekins and place on board. Serve.

# Mixed Spice, Cardamom and Lemon Cheesecake

## Ingredients – serves 4

½ packet scotch finger biscuits, crushed
20-30g melted butter
½ teaspoon mixed spice
½ teaspoon ground cardamom
½ teaspoon ground cloves

Zest and juice of 1 lemon
1 teaspoon Lemon essence
500g cream cheese, softened
2 tablespoons caster sugar
4 egg whites

## Method

Mix crushed biscuits and melted butter together and press into a lightly greased cake tin or in small tumblers.

In a large mixing bowl, add the softened cream cheese, mixed spice and ground cardamom. Beat until combined.

In another bowl, beat egg whites and caster sugar until soft peaks form. Fold into cream cheese mixture. Then fold in lemon juice.

Pour mixture into cake tin/tumblers. Keep refrigerated until ready to serve.

# Gluten and Lactose Free Chocolate and Chilli Rice Pudding

## Ingredients- serves 6

3 cups long grain rice, rinsed
600mls coconut cream
100mls water
600mls coconut milk
1 cup white sugar
160g dark Sweet William cooking chocolate
2 tablespoons dried chilli flakes
1 teaspoon vanilla essence

## Method

Combine all ingredients in a large saucepan and bring to a boil, stirring once or twice.

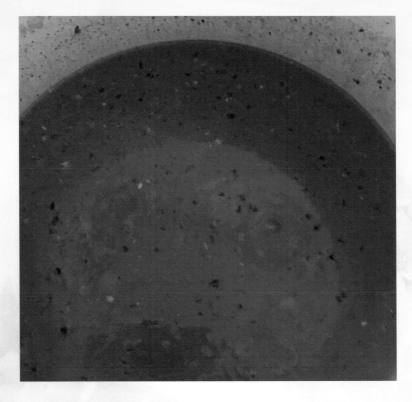

Reduce heat and simmer for 20-25 minutes, stirring occasionally.

Remove from heat and add vanilla essence.

Enjoy hot or cold.

# Pumpkin and Yam Pie

## Ingredients – serves 8

4 large vol-au-vents (175g)
2 cups of pumpkin purée (see page PUMPKIN AND YAM PUREE)
2 eggs, plus yolk of a third egg
½ cup firmly packed brown sugar
2 ½ teaspoons ground cinnamon
1 teaspoon ground nutmeg
½ teaspoon ground cloves
1 tablespoon lemon juice
1 ½ cups thickened cream
1 teaspoon crushed ginger

## Method

Pre-heat oven to 220°C.

Beat eggs with a wooden spoon in a large bowl. Mix in the sugar, spices and lemon juice.

Mix in the pumpkin purée and stir until combined.

Pour filling into shells and bake in pre- heated oven for approximately 15 minutes.

Cool on a wire rack for 2 hours before serving.

*Note that the pie will come out all puffed up from the leavening of the eggs. It will deflate as it cools.

# Rosewater and Lemon Trifle with Cardamom Custard and Caramelised Figs

## Ingredients – serves 4

2 figs, halved
300mls vanilla custard
85g grape flavoured jelly crystals
180-200g jam sponge cake
2 tablespoons rose water essence
1 teaspoon lemon juice
1 teaspoon lemon essence
1 ½ teaspoons ground cardamom
1 tablespoon white sugar
1 tablespoon balsamic vinegar
Pinch of salt

## Method

Make jelly crystals to instructions on box.

Mix rose water essence, lemon juice and lemon essence. Soak jam sponge into mix. Press a layer of cake into four tumblers. Refrigerate for 2-3 hours.

Whisk cardamom into vanilla custard and set aside in fridge.

Once jelly has set, spoon some into each tumbler. Poor some custard over the jelly. Repeat process until tumbler is full.

Meanwhile; mix sugar, salt and balsamic vinegar together. Place halved figs cut side down and coat all over.

In a small frypan over medium heat, place figs cut side down and cook for 3-5 minutes-until juices and sugar caramelized. Turn figs over and cook for another couple of minutes.

Place half a caramelized fig on top of each glass.

Serve